EDUCATIONAL STORY FOR KIDS ABOUT HEALTHY EATING

Eating Right to Shine Bright!

With Anne

Lily Greenfield

Illustrated by Anastasiia Sokha

Hello
dear friend!

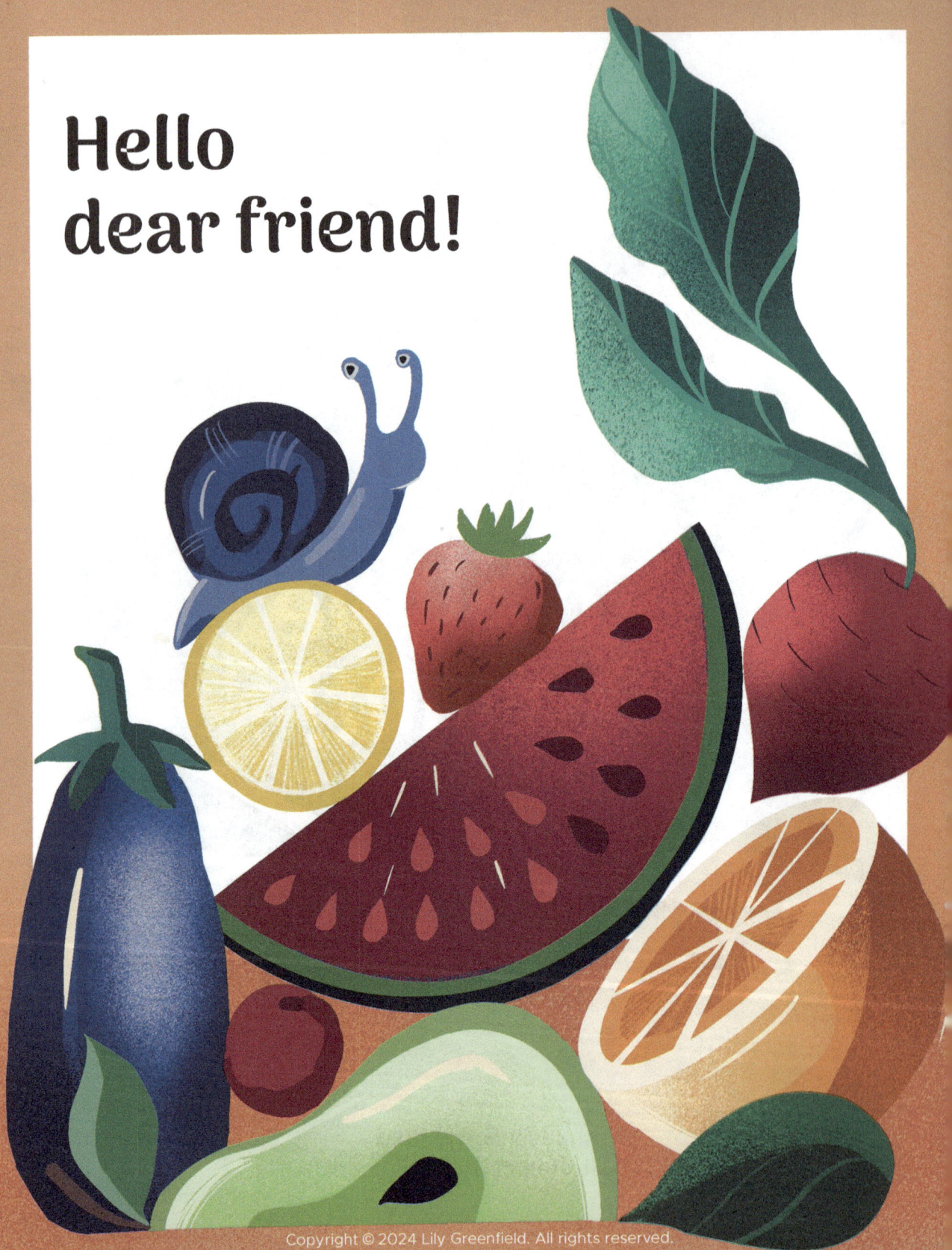

Table of Contents:

1. **Introduction:** Anne's Adventure Begins

2. **Chapter 1:** Guardian of the Magical Orchard

3. **Chapter 2:** The Great Citrus Showdown

4. **Chapter 3:** The Veggie Ball

5. **Chapter 4:** Adventures in the Exotic Jungle

6. **Chapter 5:** The Nutty Forest

7. **Chapter 6:** The Rainbow's Secret in the Fruit Garden

8. **Chapter 7:** Anne's Homecoming Feast

9. **Nutritious Garden Vocabulary**

Anne's Adventure Begins

Anne just loves exploring her garden. Every little bit of it!

But one sunny morning was different from the others. While picking yellow and red tulips to make a bouquet for her mom, she noticed something behind the giant sunflower that she was sure wasn't there before.

She crept closer. A door? Yes, it was definitely a tiny wooden door with strange carvings all over it. Curious and excited, Anne pushed open the door, never thinking twice about what could be behind it.

At first, Anne's eyes grew big as bright rainbows swirled all around her. As she looked around, the colorful lights slowly faded away. What she saw next made her gasp — a magical world full of colors and shapes she'd never seen before.

She had found the Nutritious Kingdom!

The air sparkled with sweet and fresh scents, tickling Anne's nose. Bright fruits, each with its own unique color and shape, hung from trees, and lush vegetables, some tall and leafy, others round and plump, grew from the ground.

Everywhere Anne looked, cheerful, talking fruits and veggies welcomed her with smiles!

Am I dreaming?

She saw apples as red as rubies, carrots as bright as the sun, and blueberries as blue as the sky.

Anne took a deep breath, her eyes wide with wonder as the magic of this new place tingled through her. She saw a rainbow of colors, heard the gentle rustling of leaves, and felt the soft, cool breeze. The ground beneath her feet was covered in a soft green carpet of grass, and tiny flowers dotted everything with splashes of color.

As she walked deeper into the kingdom, Anne noticed that the fruits and vegetables were not just talking but also playing games and having fun.

She saw a group of strawberries, their red bodies glistening in the sunlight, chasing each other. "They're playing tag!"

A bunch of sunny and happy bananas, their yellow skins, were swinging from the trees, having so much fun! And a family of tomatoes, their round bodies a deep shade of red, were having a picnic in the sunshine.

Everywhere Anne looked, there was something new and surprising to see.

She couldn't wait to explore more and learn more about this enchanting kingdom where fruits and vegetables came to life.

Little did she know, she was about to discover all about yummy, healthy eating, and the power of fruits and vegetables.

And so Anne's nutritious and delicious adventure began...

Chapter 1:

Guardian of the Magical Orchard

Anne's eyes sparkled as she stepped into a world of wonder. Trees laden with shimmering apples stretched as far as she could see, their leaves whispering secrets in the breeze.

"Wow!" Anne breathed, her voice filled with awe. "This is apple-solutely amazing!"

Suddenly, a gleaming red apple with twinkling eyes and a leafy crown rolled up to her. "Welcome, young adventurer!" he announced in a voice as crisp as a fall morning.

"I am Crispin, Guardian of the Nutritious Kingdom and protector of this Magical Orchard!"

Anne's jaw dropped. "A talking apple? And you're a guardian? This is the coolest thing ever!"

Crispin chuckled, his laugh sounding like apples tumbling in a basket. "Oh, I'm more than just a talking apple, my dear. I'm here to introduce you to the magical world of healthy foods!"

He waved his leaf-arm, and suddenly, tiny sparkles danced around them. "You see, Anne, you've entered the Nutritious Kingdom, a place where every fruit and vegetable has special powers to make you strong, smart, and full of energy!"

Anne's eyes widened. "Really? What kind of powers?"

Crispin puffed up proudly. "Well, we apples are just the beginning! In this kingdom, you'll find fruits and veggies of all kinds, each with its own unique gifts. Some give you super strength, others make your brain extra sharp, and some even help protect you from getting sick!"

"Wow!" Anne exclaimed. "I can't wait to explore!"

Crispin's eyes twinkled. "That's the spirit! But before you go, I have a special gift for you." He reached up to a nearby branch and plucked the most perfect, shiny apple Anne had ever seen. It sparkled like a ruby in the sunlight.

"This magical apple will give you the strength and energy you need for your adventure," Crispin explained. "Remember, Anne, eating various fruits and vegetables is the key to unlocking all their amazing powers. The more colors you eat, the more superpowers you get!" Anne took the apple, feeling its weight in her hand. As she bit into it, a wave of energy surged through her body. She felt like she could run faster than the wind and leap higher than the trees!

Eating an apple can give you a burst of energy. It is packed with natural sugars and **fiber**[1], which keep you feeling full.

[1], page 66

"Wow! I feel incredible!" Anne exclaimed, doing a little dance of joy.

Crispin nodded sagely. "That's the magic of healthy eating, Anne. And there's so much more to discover! The Nutritious Kingdom is full of wonders, each fruit and vegetable with its own special power. Are you ready for more adventures?"

Anne's eyes shone with excitement. "You bet I am! Thank you, Crispin!"

Crispin smiled warmly. "Remember, Anne, the path through our kingdom will lead you to many new friends.

Each one will teach you something special about staying healthy and strong. Now go, brave adventurer, and discover the magic of the Nutritious Kingdom!"

With a wave of her new apple friend, Anne set off down the path, clutching her magical apple and brimming with excitement. She couldn't wait to see what other amazing fruits and vegetables she would meet on her journey through this beautiful, healthy world!

Here's a fun fact:

Did you know that there are over 7,500 different types of apples in the world? Each one has its own unique flavor and color!

Chapter 2:

The Great Citrus Showdown

Anne followed a sweet, citrusy scent through the Nutritious Kingdom until she arrived at the zesty Citrus Grove. The trees were bursting with orange oranges, yellow lemons, green limes, and yellow grapefruits, all shining in the sunlight.

Wow... I really feel like taking a bite...

As Anne wandered through the grove, she noticed a group of citrus fruits chatting together. It looked serious! Ollie Orange, Lily Lemon, Levi Lime, and Gus Grapefruit were arguing over who was the healthiest citrus fruit.

"Vitamin C is what makes oranges the best!" Ollie Orange said proudly.

"But lemons are great for digestion and keeping your skin glowing!" Lily Lemon added as the argument continued to unfold.

"Limes are packed with antioxidants and help **detoxify**[2] the body," Levi Lime argued.

Gus Grapefruit, who had been grumpy before, now looked thoughtful. "Grapefruits are rich in vitamins and fiber, and are great for heart health," he said, trying to keep his temper in check.

Anne walked up to them and smiled. "Hello, everyone! This place smells amazing. What's going on here?"

"Hi, Anne!" Ollie Orange called out. "We're just discussing who the healthiest citrus fruit is."

Anne laughed. "You all sound pretty healthy to me! Can you tell me more about each of you?"

"Sure!" Ollie Orange said. "Oranges are full of **vitamin C**[3], which helps keep your **immune system**[4] strong, meaning you don't get sick often, and it keeps your skin healthy."

Lily Lemon added, "Lemons are great for adding flavor to food and drinks, and they also help with digestion and keep your skin glowing, and good for colds, too."

[2,3,4,5] page 66, 67

Levi Lime said, "Limes are high in **antioxidants**[5] and helpful for detoxifying the body!"

Gus Grapefruit, now less grumpy, said, "Grapefruits are rich in vitamins and fiber, which are great for heart health."

Anne listened, fascinated by all the information. Suddenly, Gus Grapefruit smiled and said, "Anne, I'd love to introduce you to more members of our citrus family. There's lots more of us. Follow me!"

Gus Grapefruit led Anne to a special part of the grove where even more citrus fruits were growing. As they walked, Gus began to introduce each one:

Did you know that grapefruit got its name because it grows in clusters like grapes? Imagine a bunch of tiny grapefruits hanging together just like a bunch of grapes!

Tangerines:

Easy to peel, sweet and small.
It's a perfect snack, enjoyed by all.
Packed with goodness, cute and tiny
a juicy burst for you and me!

Lemons:

Zesty and bright, full of cheer,
they're great for the skin, I hear.
Add a slice for a sunny touch,
and for your health, they mean so much.

Limes:

Tart and green, fresh and clean,
help digestion and keep you keen.
In your water, a twist of zest,
will keep you feeling at your best.

Grapefruits:

Tangy and pink, a healthy treat
for your heart, can't be beat.
A morning bite to start your day
will keep any sickness far away.

Pomelos:

Big and bold, rich and grand,
full of nutrients from sunny lands.
Slice a piece, enjoy the taste,
healthy bites, no time to waste.

Oranges:

Sweet and juicy, vitamin C,
it boosts your health, as you can see.
It keeps your body feeling right,
every bite will delight!

Anne's brain buzzed with all the juicy new information. Then, because she couldn't wait a minute more, she tasted each citrus fruit, her face scrunching up with the sour ones and relaxing into a smile with the sweet ones. Each bite was like a little healthy adventure for her taste buds!

"These are so good!" Anne exclaimed. "Thank you, Gus Grapefruit, for showing me all these amazing citrus fruits."

"You're welcome, Anne," Gus Grapefruit said proudly. "We're glad you enjoyed learning about our citrus family."

Anne smiled and picked a ripe orange from a tree. She peeled it and tasted the juicy segments. The sweet and tangy flavor instantly refreshed her and filled her with a burst of energy, making her feel cheery and healthy.

"Thank you, Ollie Orange, Lily Lemon, Levi Lime, and last but not least, Gus Grapefruit! I've learned so much about how good citrus fruits are for you," Anne said, her voice filled with a sense of accomplishment and happiness.

"I loved trying them too!" As Anne thanked her new friends and prepared to leave Citrus Grove, Gus Grapefruit said, "Anne, just ahead, you'll find the Veggie Terrace. Our friends there will have some more unique benefits to share." With newfound energy and a head full of citrusy knowledge, Anne waved goodbye.

Chapter 3:

The Veggie Ball

As she walked, lively music and laughter reached her ears. That's interesting! She thought and followed the sounds and soon arrived at a grand celebration — a Veggie Ball!

Colorful banners made of leaves and flowers hung between the trees, and a happy tune filled the air. Vegetables of all kinds were dancing and having a wonderful time. In the center of it all was Betty Brocolli, leading the party with a big smile.

"Welcome to the Veggie Ball!" Betty Brocolli called out to Anne, waving her over. "We're so glad you could join us!"

Anne's eyes sparkled. "This is amazing! What's the Veggie Ball?"

Just then, a carrot hopped over and introduced himself.

"Hi, Anne! I'm Carl Carrot, and I'm packed with **beta-carotene[6],** which helps you see in the dark and keeps your skin nice and healthy!"

[6] page 67

Anne smiled at Carl. "Nice to meet you, Carl!"

Carl Carrot grinned. "Well, you've already met our superstar, Betty Brocolli. She's the one who organized this magical celebration."

Betty Broccoli flexed her little florets and said, "I have many vitamins that keep your bones strong and help your tummy feel good. I also have special things that can keep you from getting sick! Let me tell you a story about how I became a superstar..."

Anne listened as Betty Brocolli continued, "Once upon a time, I was just a tiny broccoli sprout in a big garden," Betty Brocolli began, her eyes shining.

"I dreamed of becoming a superstar, but I didn't know how. One day, a group of kids came to visit the garden. They looked at me and said, 'Eww, broccoli!' I felt so sad!"

Anne listened, her curiosity growing. "But then," Betty Broccoli continued, "A wise old tomato named Tommy told me, 'Betty Brocolli, don't you know you have superpowers? Your vitamins can make kids as strong as superheroes!'

So, I decided to show them my superpowers. I started flexing my florets and showing off my green, leafy strength."

Anne giggled at the thought of Betty Brocolli flexing her florets.

"One brave little boy named Timmy decided to give me a try. He took a bite and exclaimed, 'Wow, this broccoli is awesome!' Soon, all the kids ate broccoli and felt super strong and healthy. They even raced, and guess what? Timmy won because he had eaten so much broccoli!"

"That's incredible!" said Anne, wanting to take a bite of Betty Broccoli herself.

Betty nodded proudly. "From that day on, I became known as Betty Broccoli, the veggie with superpowers. And now I help kids discover their superpowers by eating healthy vegetables everywhere." "That's so cool!" Anne exclaimed. "You really are a superstar!"

Betty Broccoli grinned and looked around. "Would you like to meet more of our veggie friends?"

"Yes, please!" Anne said. Betty Broccoli led Anne around the clearing, where she met more veggie friends:

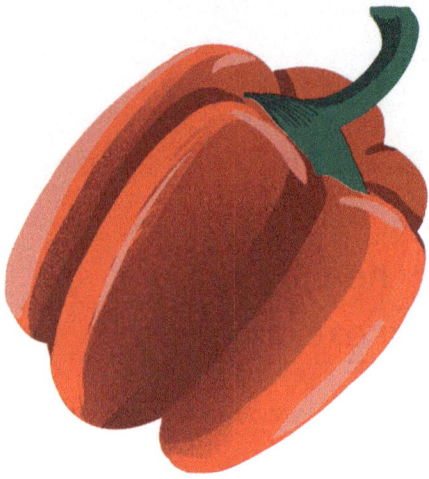

Bell Pepper:

Vitamin C for a glowing face,
strong and healthy,
full of grace.

Cucumber:

A refreshing treat
for the kin and tummy,
cool and crisp, always yummy.

Beet:

Vitamins help your blood to flow.
With an energizing boost,
you will glow.

Tomato:

It has **lycopene**[7] for a happy heart, for living a healthy life is a vital part.

Garlic:

Keeps your body strong every time, just a little clove works overtime.

Zucchini:

A **vitamin A**[8] and **potassium**[9] blend, for your health, they know how to defend.

Corn:

Golden kernels filled with fiber's might, good for your tummy and your sight.

Cauliflower:

Vitamins C and **K**[10] keep your bones strong, you'll be healthy all day long.

Potato:

Rich in potassium and vitamin C, fueling you with energy.

[7,8,9,10] **page 67,68**

Here's a fun fact:

⭐ Did you know that carrots were originally purple, red, and yellow? The orange carrot we know today was developed in the Netherlands in the 17th century!

Anne was stunned by all the different types of vegetables dancing around her, each one proudly sharing its special benefits. As she danced with Betty Broccoli and twirled with Zoe Zucchini, she felt a sense of joy and health fill her right up.

Suddenly, Betty Broccoli clapped her hands to get everyone's attention. "Friends, let's gather for a special moment! Anne has joined us today, and we want to share our veggie wisdom with her."

The veggies gathered around Anne, and she listened as each one shared its benefits. She felt grateful for the new knowledge and the fun party.

"Thank you, Betty Broccoli, Carl Carrot, and all my new veggie friends! I've learned so much about how vegetables are so good for me," Anne said gratefully.

Betty Broccoli stepped forward with a proud smile. "Anne, there's an exciting place just ahead — the Exotic Jungle. You'll meet amazing new fruits there!"

Anne happily waved goodbye to her veggie friends, about to continue her adventure to the Exotic Jungle in the Nutritious Kingdom.

Chapter 4:

Adventures in the Exotic Jungle

Anne wandered further along the winding path after saying goodbye to her veggie friends at the Veggie Terrace. Many twists and turns later, she found herself in a lush and active jungle. It was warm, and the air was thick with the sweet scent of tropical fruits, and birds chirped happily.

As Anne ventured deeper into the jungle, she could hardly see the tops of the towering trees dripping with fruits she'd never seen before. Just then, Max Mango swung down from the branches. "Hello, Anne! Welcome to the Exotic Jungle! I'm Max Mango, and I'll guide you through this fruity paradise."

Anne smiled. "Hi, Max Mango! This place is so cool! I've never seen so many exotic fruits before."

Max Mango grinned and said, "Let me show you around and introduce you to some of my fruity friends. By the way, mangoes like me are high in vitamin C and A, which help your immunity so that you don't get sick and keep your skin healthy."

As they walked through the jungle, Max pointed out various fruits on the trees. "Meet Patty Pineapple," he said, pointing to a spiky, golden fruit. "Pineapples are full of vitamin C, which helps keep your immune system strong, and **enzymes**[11] that help digestion."

Avocados are also known as 'alligator pears' because of their pear shape and bumpy green skin. They are superfoods packed with healthy fats that give you energy and help your brain work better!

[11] **page 68**

Patty Pineapple waved her leafy top and said,
"Plus, I'm super sweet and juicy! Perfect for a hot day."

Next, they came across a group of bright green fruits.
"This is Katie Kiwi," Max introduced. "Kiwis are small but
mighty, packed with vitamin C, K, and fiber, which are great
for boosting immunity and aiding digestion."

Katie Kiwi rolled over and added, "And I've got a tangy
flavor that's both sweet and refreshing!"

As they continued, Anne noticed a large, smooth-skinned
fruit. "Who's that?" she asked.

"That's Abby Avocado," Max Mango replied. "Avocados
are rich in healthy fats, which give you energy and keep your
heart healthy, and vitamin C, which helps your body heal."

Abby Avocado smiled and said, "I'm also delicious in salads
and on toast!"

Further along, they met Ben Banana hanging from a tall
tree. "Hello, Anne! Bananas are a great source of potassium,
which helps your muscles work well, and for energy,"
Ben Banana said cheerfully. "They're perfect
for a quick snack!"

Anne loved hearing all about the different fruits. But the best part was when she tasted each fruit, one by one, enjoying its unique flavors and textures.

"These are incredible!" Anne exclaimed. I feel so energized and healthy!"

"Wait, Anne! There's more!" Max Mango led her to a colorful patch where other fruits were growing.

As they walked, Max Mango led Anne to a clearing where a fruity festival occurred. Each fruit had a role to play, and they all crowded around to celebrate the wonders of the Exotic Jungle.

Suddenly, a playful parrot flew overhead and dropped a coconut from the sky. "Oops, sorry!" squawked Coco the Parrot. "I just wanted to join the fun!"

Max Mango laughed and introduced Anne to Coco. "This is Coco, our mischievous Parrot. He loves coconuts, which are full of electrolytes. **Electrolytes**[12] are like little helpers that keep your body **hydrated**[13] and energetic."

Coco perched on a branch and sang a little rhyme: "If you're feeling flat, never fear, coconuts hydrate, energize, and are full of cheer!"

Anne giggled and clapped her hands, delighted by the playful Parrot. "That's so fun, Coco!" Max Mango then pointed out some more exotic fruits, each with its own special benefits:

[12,13] **page 68**

Mangoes:

High in vitamins C and A,
they will keep your health
and skin okay.

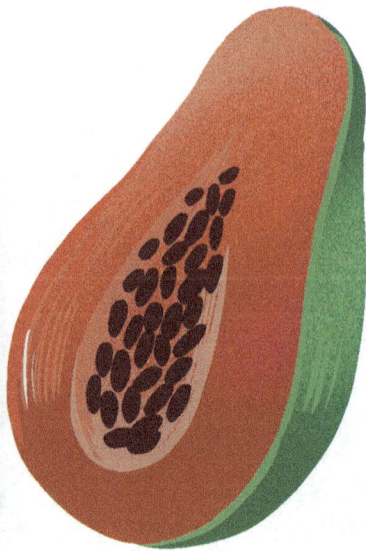

Papayas:

With vitamins C and E in store,
they keep your tummy
from feeling sore.

Coconuts:

Full of electrolytes and healthy fat,
you can hydrate and energize
just like that.

Dragon Fruits:

With antioxidants
and vitamin C,
they keep you feeling
super healthy.

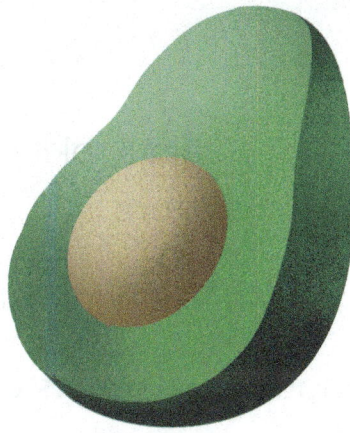

Avocados:

Healthy fats
and vitamins for you,
a boost for your heart
and skin, too.

Passion Fruits:

Their vitamins A
and vitamin C
make your eyes
and skin healthy.

Kiwis:

With vitamins C and K,
they're pretty grand,
nature's snack
at your command.

Guavas:

Packed with vitamin C,
so sweet,
with immunity boosts,
they are a treat.

Pineapples:

With enzymes
and vitamin C,
they are a digestion
superstar.

"Wow...I love them all!" Anne said, looking at each one with its unique shape, color, and texture.

"Thank you, Max Mango, and all my new fruity friends!

I've learned so much about the benefits of exotic fruits," Anne said.

Max Mango, "Anne, keep walking forward, and you'll find the Nutty Forest. You'll meet some amazing nuts there!"

Anne waved goodbye to her fruity friends. She couldn't wait to check out the Nutty Forest and meet more wonderful friends in the Nutritious Garden.

Here's a fun fact:

Dragon fruit, also known as pitaya, grows on a type of cactus! Its bright pink or yellow skin with green scales makes it look like a dragon. Inside, it's filled with tiny black seeds and sweet, juicy flesh that can be white, pink, or even red.

This exotic fruit is not only delicious but also packed with vitamins and antioxidants, making it a superfood that's great for your health!

Chapter 5:

The Nutty Forest

Anne followed the winding path from the Exotic Jungle again and quickly found herself in a new area called the Nutty Forest. The air was filled with the rich, earthy scent of nuts, and the surrounding trees carried clusters of almonds, walnuts, peanuts, and cashews. Yum! The forest felt alive with the gentle rustling of leaves and the whispers of nature.

Anne spotted a happy-looking almond waving at her as she walked through the forest.

"Hello, Anne! Welcome to the Nutty Forest!" Andy Almond called out.

"Hi, Andy Almond! I've never seen so many nuts!

What can you tell me about them all?"

Andy Almond grinned. "Nuts are full of healthy things that keep your body strong. Let me introduce you to my friends, and they can tell you more."

Andy Almond led Anne deeper into the forest, where they found Wendy Walnut collecting fallen nuts.

"Hi, Anne! I'm Wendy Walnut. Walnuts are great for your brain and heart because they have something called **omega-3 fatty acids**[14]."

Anne looked curious. "Omega-3 fatty acids? What are those?"

Wendy Walnut smiled. "Omega-3 fatty acids are like tiny helpers for your brain and heart. They keep your mind sharp so you can learn and remember things and keep your heart healthy so you can play and run."

Next, Anne met Pete Peanut, who was bouncing around. "Hi, Anne! I'm Pete. Peanuts are packed with protein, which helps you build strong muscles and keeps you full of energy. Like me!"

Finally, Andy Almond took Anne to meet Casey Cashew who was arranging cashews into neat piles.

"Hello, Anne! Cashews have lots of magnesium, which helps your bones stay strong and your nerves work well."

Anne was fascinated by all the beautiful things she was learning. "Wow! I had no idea that nuts were so amazing! Are there more nuts here?"

[14] **page 69**

Andy Almond laughed. "Just you wait! I'll show you more of our nutty friends and their benefits."

They walked to a new part of the forest where Anne saw lots of different nut trees. Andy Almond pointed them out one by one, each with a bit of rhyme to help Anne remember their benefits:

Eating almonds can help you think better and stay sharp because they are great for brain health.

Almonds:

They have Vitamin E[15],
a radiant skin treat,
making it glowy and soft,
a beauty complete.

Walnuts:

There's Omega-3s
with every crunch,
for your brain and heart,
pop them in your lunch.

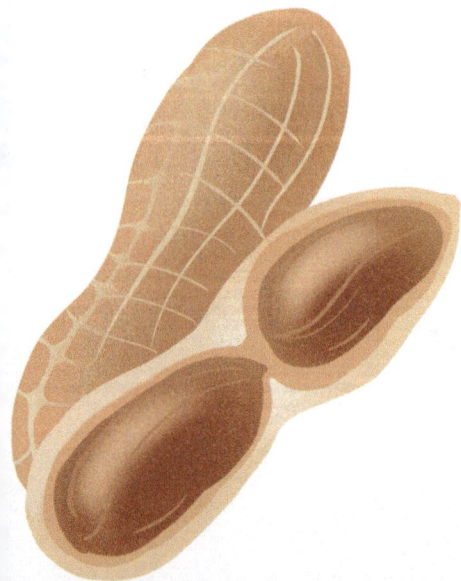

Peanuts:

With **protein**[16] power,
to make muscles strong,
they will boost your energy
all day long.

Cashews:

Magnesium keeps
bones so strong,
so you won't need
to rest for too long.

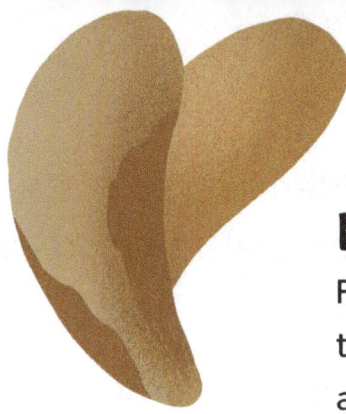

Brazil Nuts:

Full of **Selenium**[17]
to keep you strong,
and immunity that
will be lifelong.

Pistachios:

Fiber-rich,
they're digestion's friend,
leaving you feeling full
till the day's end.

Pecans:

They have antioxidants
to protect,
they're your body's
guard from any defect.

Hazelnuts:

With vitamin E
and healthy fats,
your heart will thank you
for all that.

Macadamia:

Healthy fats
for the heart and mind,
with energy and strength
combined.

[15,16,17] **page 69**

Anne tried a few different types of nuts. Each had its unique shape, color, and texture! The more she learned, the more excited she became.

"These nuts are incredible!" Anne exclaimed.
"I feel healthier just being here with you all."

"Thank you, Anne," Andy Almond said.
"We're glad you enjoyed learning about our nutty family."

Wendy Walnut added, "Just ahead, you'll see the Fruit Garden. You'll meet amazing new fruits there!"

Anne waved goodbye to her nutty friends and continued her journey, eager to discover the Fruit Garden and meet more wonderful friends in the Nutritious Kingdom.

Here's a fun fact:

Did you know that cashews grow on the bottom of cashew apples? These kidney-shaped seeds are packed with nutrients like magnesium, which helps keep your bones strong, and healthy fats that are great for your heart. Plus, they're super creamy and delicious!

Chapter 6:

The Rainbow's Secret in the Fruit Garden

After leaving the Nutty Forest, Anne followed a sunny path to the Fruit Garden. The trees were heavy with colorful, juicy fruits, and the air was filled with the sweet fragrance of ripe fruit. But I thought I'd seen all the fruits! Wondered Anne.

As Anne wandered through the garden, she noticed an unusual sight — a rainbow stretching across the sky, ending at a cluster of fruit trees. Curious, Anne decided to follow the rainbow's path. As she got closer, she saw a sign that read, "Welcome to the Fruit Garden's Rainbow Hunt!"

A rainbow hunt? This sounds like fun!" she exclaimed.

It wasn't long before Anne stumbled upon a large basket. What's this? She wondered. It was filled with colorful fruit-shaped clues. Anne picked up the first clue, shaped like a cherry, and read it aloud:

"Find Charlie Cherry, who loves to dance. He's waiting for you, so take a chance!"

Anne giggled and began her search. She soon found Charlie Cherry twirling under a cherry tree.

"Hello, Anne! I'm Charlie Cherry. Cherries are full of antioxidants and vitamins that help keep you healthy and strong."

Charlie Cherry handed Anne another clue, this one shaped like a grape. Anne read the clue:

"Gary Grape is next, hanging on a vine.
He'll tell you why grapes are so fine!"

Anne hurried over to a vine full of glistening grapes and found Gary Grape. "Hi, Anne! Grapes are full of vitamins and antioxidants that help keep your heart healthy."

Gary Grape handed Anne the next clue, shaped like an apple. The clue read:

"Apple Abby and Pear Polly have a treat.
They'll tell you about the benefits that you eat!"

Anne found Abby Apple and Polly Pear near a cozy apple and pear grove. Abby Apple said, "I'm full of fiber and vitamin C, excellent for heart health and digestion."

Polly Pear added, "I'm high in fiber and antioxidants, good for heart health and digestion too!"

Abby Apple handed Anne another clue, this one shaped like a peach. Anne read it:

"Peggy Peach is full of delight. Find her to learn how she keeps you bright!"

The fuzzy skin on peaches isn't just there for decoration. It helps protect the fruit from insects and sunburn! This natural "sunscreen" keeps peaches safe and keeps them juicy and delicious as they grow.

Anne quickly found Peggy Peach sitting under a peach tree. "Hello, Anne! I'm rich in vitamins A and C, good for skin and eye health."

Peggy Peach handed Anne the next clue, shaped like a plum. The clue read:

"Paddy Plum is ready to share. Find him to learn about his fruity care!"

Anne spotted Paddy Plum by a plum tree. "Hi, Anne! I'm high in fiber and vitamins, great for digestion and bone health."

As Anne collected each clue, she learned fascinating facts about the fruits in the garden. She found Polly Pomegranate, Axel Apricot, Percy Persimmon, Charlie Cherry and other each sharing their unique benefits:

Here's a fun fact:

Did you know that apples can float in water? It's because apples are made up of 25% air! It makes them perfect for fun games like apple bobbing.

Apricot:

A summer fruit,
they're soft and sweet,
for eyes and skin,
they are a treat.

Banana:

Golden and bright,
a sunny delight,
potassium-rich,

for strength and might.

Persimmon:

Fiber-filled,
aiding digestion with care,
for healthy eyes and a tummy,
it is always there.

Cherry:

With vitamins A and C,
inflammation they fight,
supporting heart health,
making everything right.

Apple:

Orchard's treasure,
crisp and sweet,
an apple a day,
they're hard to beat.

Peach:

Blushing and soft,
summer's sweet kiss.
Vitamins for the skin and
eyes are pure bliss.

Pomegranate:

Jewels of red,
with antioxidants to fight,
for heart and health,
they're powerful, alright.

Plum:

High in fiber,
and for bones
they're pretty neat,
 they keep digestion
to a happy beat.

Pear:

Gentle and sweet,
they're nature's embrace,
and with vitamins and fiber,
they put a smile
on your face.

Finally, Anne found the last clue, shaped like a golden fruit. It read: "Find the Rainbow Tree, where all fruits unite. It's time to celebrate the magic of each bite!"

Anne followed the rainbow to the Rainbow Tree, a magnificent tree with fruits of every color hanging from its branches.

Chi Chi, the squirrel, was waiting for her.

"Congratulations, Anne! You've completed the Rainbow Hunt and discovered the magic of the Fruit Garden!"

Chi and the fruits crowded around Anne and began singing and dancing, celebrating her incredible journey. Anne felt a warm glow of happiness in her tummy as she danced with her fruity friends.

As the celebration ended, Anne, with the biggest grin on her face, waved goodbye to her fruity friends. Walking back down the path, she heard a voice calling..."Anne, Anne!" It was her mother's voice calling her name in the distance. The sound grew louder and more familiar, gently pulling her from her slumber. Anne slowly opened her eyes, feeling the sun's warmth on her face and the soft rustling of leaves above. She found herself lying under a tree in her garden, the familiar sights and sounds of home surrounding her. Oh, was it all a dream? She wondered, smiling as the magic of her adventure lingered in her heart.

Chapter 7:

Anne's Homecoming Feast

Anne's eyes fluttered open, sunbeams dancing through the leaves above her. She yawned, stretching her arms wide, when suddenly – "Whoa!" She tumbled backward, nearly knocked over by a gigantic basket that had magically appeared. The basket brimmed with the most vibrant fruits and veggies Anne had ever seen, some even glowing softly as if touched by fairy dust!

"No way!" Anne gasped memories of her fantastic journey rushing back. She hugged the basket tight and dashed into the house, leaving a trail of bouncing apples in her wake.

"Mom! Dad!" Anne shouted, sliding into the kitchen. "You'll never believe where I've been!" Her parents' eyes widened at the sight of Anne, leaves tangled in her hair, clutching an enormous basket of produce.

"I visited the Nutritious Kingdom!" Anne announced, hopping with excitement. As she recounted her adventure, the fruits and veggies in the basket seemed to perk up as if reliving the tale alongside her.

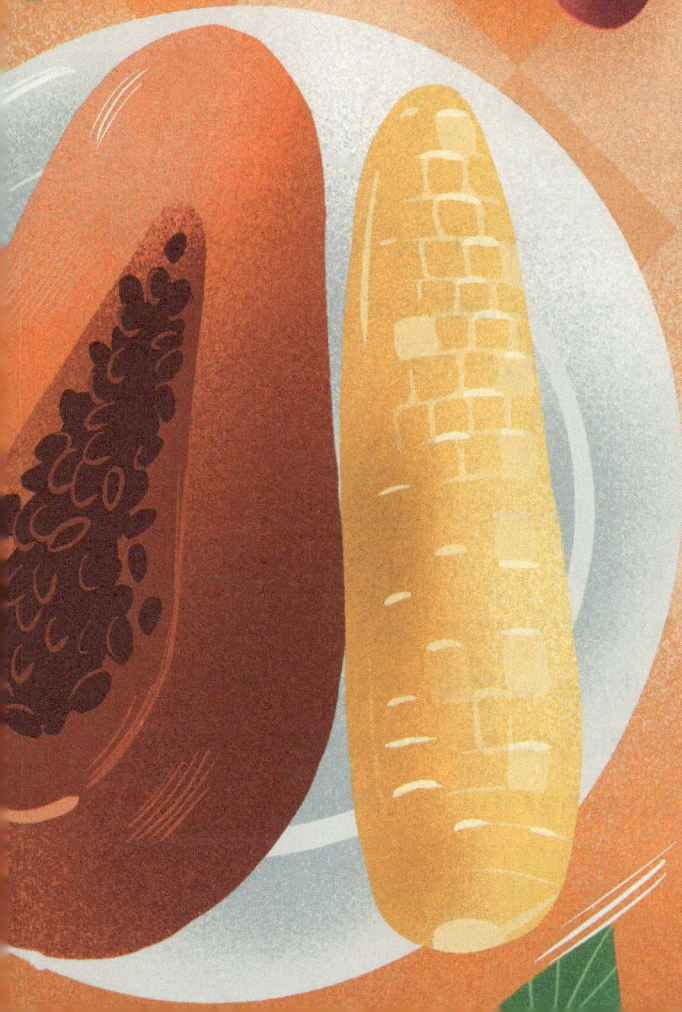

Her dad chuckled, dodging a flying carrot. "Wow, sweetie! It sounds like you've become a real food expert!"

"I have!" Anne nodded eagerly. "Every fruit and veggie has its own superpower. It's like eating a team of tiny, tasty superheroes!"Anne's mom grinned, "Well, why don't we put these superheroes to work? Let's create the most magical dinner ever!"

"Yes!" Anne cheered, swiftly tying on her favorite apron.

The kitchen transformed into a colorful whirlwind of chopping, mixing, and laughter. Anne shared fun facts as they cooked, explaining that peaches have fuzzy skin that protects them from insects and sunburn.

Soon, the table was set with a feast that looked like a rainbow had painted their plates. Green salads sat next to exotic fruit smoothies while a stir-fry sizzled with all the vibrant colors of Veggie Valley.

As they savored their meal, Anne regaled her parents with more tales of her adventure. The broccoli florets on her plate seemed to nod as if confirming every word. As Anne snuggled into bed that night, she felt her whole body buzzing with health and happiness. She closed her eyes, wondering what magical adventures awaited her in her dreams and beyond.

Nutritious Garden Vocabulary

Here you'll find fun and detailed explanations for some of the unique words Anne learned on her adventure. Let's dive in and discover the magic behind these words!

1. Fiber:

Fiber is a type of carbohydrate that your body cannot digest. It helps keep your digestive system healthy by moving food through your stomach and intestines smoothly.

2. Detoxification

Detoxification is the process of removing harmful substances from the body. Some foods, like limes and leafy greens, help the body detoxify by supporting the liver and kidneys.

3. Vitamin C

Vitamin C is an essential nutrient that helps keep your skin glows and boosts your immune system.

4. Immune System

Your immune system is like a shield that protects you from germs and infections, helping you stay healthy.

5. Antioxidants

Antioxidants are like tiny superheroes inside your body. They protect your cells from getting damaged by fighting off harmful things called free radicals. Free radicals can make you sick, but antioxidants keep you healthy and strong. You can find antioxidants in colorful fruits and vegetables like blueberries, strawberries, and carrots. They help you stay healthy and feel great!

6. Beta-Carotene

Beta-carotene is a nutrient that your body turns into vitamin A. It helps keep your eyes healthy, your immune system strong, and your skin glowing.

7. Lycopene

Lycopene is a powerful antioxidant found in red and pink fruits like tomatoes, watermelon, and grapefruit. It helps protect your cells from damage and support heart health.

8. Vitamin A

Vitamin A helps you see better in the dark and strengthens your immune system.

9. Potassium

Potassium is a mineral that helps your muscles work properly and keeps your heart healthy.

10. Vitamin K

Vitamin K is essential for helping your blood clot when you get a cut and keeping your bones strong.

11. Enzymes

Enzymes are special proteins that help speed up chemical reactions in your body, including digestion. They help break down food into smaller pieces so your body can use the nutrients more efficiently.

12. Electrolytes

Electrolytes are minerals that help keep your body hydrated and your muscles working correctly.

13. Hydration

Hydration means supplying your body with enough water to stay healthy and function properly. Drinking enough water helps you stay energized, keeps your skin glowing, and ensures that your body can perform all its important tasks.

14. Omega-3 Fatty Acids

Omega-3 fatty acids are healthy fats that are really good for your brain and heart. They help your brain work better, improve your memory, and keep your heart strong and healthy.

15. Vitamin E

Vitamin E is like a shield for your cells, protecting them from getting hurt. It also helps your immune system, which is your body's way of staying strong and fighting off germs.

16. Protein

Protein, often referred to as the building blocks of the body, is instrumental in repairing and maintaining strong muscles. It also aids in the recovery of injured body parts, thereby contributing to overall health and well-being.

17. Selenium

Selenium is like a special little helper for your body. It protects your cells from getting hurt and keeps your immune system strong so you don't get sick. Selenium also helps your body work properly and keeps your hair and nails healthy.

Now it's your turn! Draw your favorite fruits and vegetables and share what you love about them. Which ones are your superheroes for staying healthy and strong?

Made in the USA
Las Vegas, NV
22 September 2024